KIMIKO MURAKAMI

KIMIKO

HERITAGE

Trailblazing Canadians

MURAKAMI

A JAPANESE-CANADIAN PIONEER

WRITTEN BY

HALEY HEALEY

ILLUSTRATED BY

KIMIKO FRASER

Heritage House Publishing Company Ltd.
heritagehouse.ca

Cataloguing information available from Library and Archives Canada
978-1-77203-431-8 (hardcover)
978-1-77203-467-7 (paperback)
978-1-77203-432-5 (ebook)

Illustrated by Kimiko Fraser
Cover and interior book design by Setareh Ashrafologhalai

The interior of this book was produced on FSC®-certified, acid-free paper,
processed chlorine free, and printed with vegetable-based inks.

Heritage House gratefully acknowledges that the land on which we live
and work is within the traditional territories of the Lkwungen (Esquimalt
and Songhees), Malahat, Pacheedaht, Scia'new, T'Sou-ke, and
W̱SÁNEĆ (Pauquachin, Tsartlip, Tsawout, Tseycum) Peoples.

We acknowledge the financial support of the Government of Canada through
the Canada Book Fund (CBF) and the Canada Council for the Arts, and
the Province of British Columbia through the British
Columbia Arts Council and the Book Publishing Tax Credit.

27 26 25 24 23   1 2 3 4 5

Printed in China

Illustrations inspired by original images courtesy of: The Murakami Family photo collection
held at the Salt Spring Island Archives (https://saltspringarchives.com/Murakami_Family/
index.html); City of Vancouver Archives (CVA 180-3516, CVA 1184-10, CVA 1184-12,
CVA 99-4619, and 2011-092.4960); and Nikkei National Museum (images 2010.
23.2.4.138, 2019.17.2.9.201, 1996.178.1.36, 2019.17.2.10.302, and 2011.79.4.1.4.40).

The author and illustrator wish to thank the family of Kimiko Murakami, especially Mary Kitagawa, for her careful review of the manuscript and support for this book.

NOTE OF TRUTH AND RECONCILIATION

This book was written on the traditional territory of the Snuneymuxw First Nation. Some of the story takes place on the traditional territory of the Saanich (W̱SÁNEĆ), Cowichan (Quw'utsun), and Chemainus (Stz'uminus) First Nations. The author fully and completely supports truth and reconciliation and recognizes her own role in truth and reconciliation.

KIMIKO was born in a coastal village outside of Vancouver. When she was five years old, she and her family moved to nearby Salt Spring Island.

Kimiko's family were fishers, then farmers. They raised chickens and grew tomatoes, berries, and other fruits and vegetables. They sold them to fancy places like the Empress Hotel in Victoria.

Kimiko was one of the first women on Salt Spring Island to learn how to drive. She drove her family's truck to buy chicken feed and to sell chicken eggs to the island store.

When Kimiko grew up, she married a man named Katsuyori. They had five children: Alice (Atsuko), Violet (Taeko), Mary (Keiko), Rose (Takako), and Richard (Katsuhide). Bruce (Yorihide) was born a few years later. The family continued to work on the farm, growing fruits and vegetables and raising chickens. It was a good life.

But everything changed during the Second World War. Canada made new and unfair rules for Japanese Canadians. A ship called the *Princess Mary* took all people of Japanese heritage to Vancouver. This included Kimiko and her family.

When the ship arrived in Vancouver, Kimiko and her family were taken to a place called Hastings Park. They were put in areas made for animals, called barns. The barns had no indoor toilets or running water. Kimiko and her children were not allowed to leave.

Many Japanese Canadians were held at Hastings Park for a while, before being sent to other places called internment camps. Like Kimiko's family, these people had done nothing wrong. They lived in Canada, and most were born in Canada. But because they had Japanese heritage, Canada made them follow the new and unfair rules.

Kimiko and her family went through difficult times. During these times, Kimiko remembered a Japanese word that helped her a lot. The word was ganbaru. It means to push on through hard times and never give up. Then and there, Kimiko decided she would have a ganbaru spirit. She would stand firm and not give up.

When Kimiko and her family were taken from Hastings Park and sent by train to an internment camp in Greenwood, British Columbia, Kimiko did not give up. And later, when they were taken to Magrath, Alberta, to work on a sugar beet farm, she *still* did not give up.

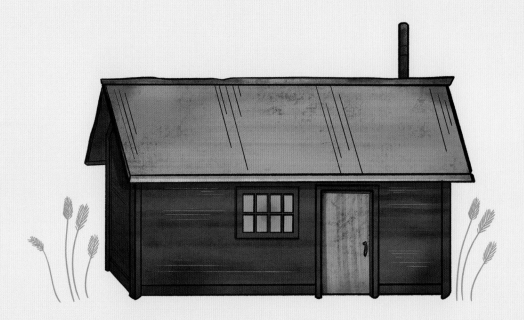

In Magrath, they lived in a small shack with no electricity and no running water. Alberta winters were snowy and much colder than BC. But Kimiko kept a ganbaru spirit, even when she and her family were forced to move yet again to a different camp in BC surrounded by tall mountains.

Years later, the war ended. The Canadian government told Kimiko's family that they could either go to Japan or go east of the Rocky Mountains. They were not prisoners anymore, but they were not allowed to return to the west coast.

Some Japanese Canadians decided go to Japan, even if they had lived in Canada their whole lives. But Kimiko kept a ganbaru spirit. She didn't want to go to Japan. Her family was determined to return to Salt Spring Island, where they had lived before the war.

So, her family opened a restaurant in Cardston, Alberta. They started saving money to return to Salt Spring Island. They saved, and saved, and saved. All the while, Kimiko kept a ganbaru spirit.

Finally, they saved up enough money and were allowed to return to their home. Kimiko and her family were the only Japanese-Canadian family to return to Salt Spring Island after the war.

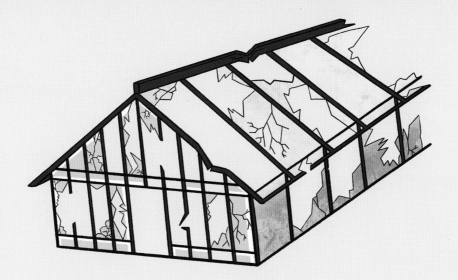

When they got there, they realized their land and belongings had been sold. The Japanese cemetery was filled with garbage.

Some people treated Kimiko and her family badly for no reason. When people treat others badly or unfairly because of the colour of their skin or where they are from, it is called racism.

But Kimiko kept a ganbaru spirit. She and her family started rebuilding everything they had lost.

They bought new land. They prepared their fields and planted more crops.

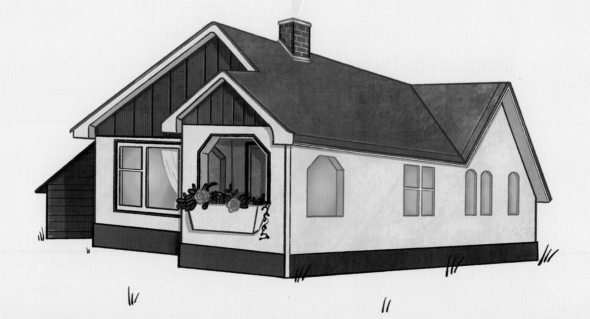

Once again, they farmed. They
sold big, shiny fruits and vegetables.
And they set to work cleaning up the
Japanese cemetery. The whole time,
Kimiko kept a ganbaru spirit.

Slowly and steadily, Kimiko and her family rebuilt the life that had been taken away from them. But they never forgot the bad years.

When Kimiko's children were fully grown, they donated some of their family's land to build homes for people going through hard times. They remembered what it was like to live in bad conditions and wanted to help others.

Today, Kimiko is remembered as a strong and amazing woman. Facing racism and injustice, Kimiko always remembered the Japanese word ganbaru and never gave up when things weren't fair and weren't right.

No matter what, Kimiko kept a ganbaru spirit.

HISTORICAL TIMELINE

1904
SEPTEMBER 25: Kimiko is born in Steveston, BC.

1926
Kimiko marries Katsuyori Murakami.

1939
SEPTEMBER 1: The Second World War begins.

SEPTEMBER 10: Canada enters the Second World War.

1941
DECEMBER 7: Japan bombs Pearl Harbour. The United States of America enters the Second World War. Canada, an ally of the United States, declares war against Japan.

1942
FEBRUARY 26: The Canadian War Measures Act declares that all people with Japanese heritage in Canada are "enemy aliens." They must move at least 161 kilometres away from coastal regions.

MARCH 4: Internment of Japanese Canadians begins. About 22,000 Japanese Canadians are interned in camps.
　During this period, until the end of the war, Kimiko and her family are sent first to Hastings Park in Vancouver (where the PNE stands today), then to an internment camp in Greenwood, BC, then to a sugar beet farm in Magrath, Alberta.

1945

SEPTEMBER 2: The Second World War ends.

The Canadian government begins to offer Japanese Canadians the choice of moving to Japan or east of the Canadian Rockies. They still do not regain their full rights and are not allowed to move to the west coast, where many had lived before the war.

Kimiko and her family choose to stay in Canada and save their money until they are able to move back to Salt Spring Island.

1954

After many years of hardship, Kimiko's family finally returns to Salt Spring Island. They are the only Japanese Canadians to do so. When they get there, they find that their land had been sold without their consent. Kimiko buys a piece of land on Rainbow Road and builds her farm and business all over again.

1949

APRIL 1: The internment policy of Japanese Canadians officially ends, although the war ended four years earlier. Japanese Canadians are once again allowed to move freely, vote, and access their rights as Canadian citizens.

1988

SEPTEMBER 22: Canadian prime minister Brian Mulroney apologizes to Japanese Canadians on behalf of the Canadian government for the internment policy. No Japanese Canadian person was ever found to be disloyal to Canada during the war, but the policy treated all Japanese Canadians as prisoners in their own country. The internment of Japanese Canadians is considered one of the worst human rights violations in Canadian history.

1997

JULY: Kimiko dies in Salt Spring Island. More than 250 islanders attend her memorial service. Kimiko is remembered for her strength, perseverance, and contributions to her community.

 HALEY HEALEY is a high school counsellor, registered clinical counsellor, and the bestselling author of *On Their Own Terms: True Stories of Trailblazing Women of Vancouver Island, Flourishing and Free: More Stories of Trailblazing Women of Vancouver Island,* and *Her Courage Rises: 50 Trailblazing Women of British Columbia and the Yukon.* A self-proclaimed trailblazing woman herself, she has taught in isolated fly-in communities, guided whitewater canoe expeditions, and is happiest outdoors. She has an avid interest in wild places and unconventional people.

 KIMIKO FRASER is an illustrator and historian-in-training. She grew up constantly making— drawing, painting, knitting, sculpting, book-binding, etc.—and has never learned how to stop. She is the illustrator of *Her Courage Rises: 50 Trailblazing Women of British Columbia and the Yukon.* She holds a bachelor of arts (honours History, major Visual Arts) from the University of Victoria. She works with many mediums to create her illustrations, including watercolour, digital, ink, and tea. Most of her work is inspired by her interest in plants, history, and folktales.